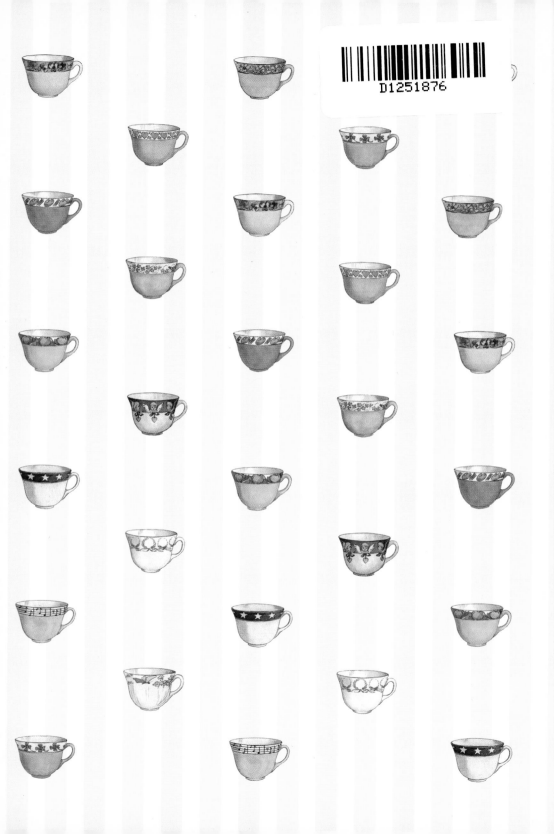

Children's
TEATIME

Children's TEATIME

By
DEBORAH
THOMAS

GREEN TIGER PRESS · MMVIII

ISBN 978-1-59583-288-7

GREEN TIGER PRESS
A DIVISION OF LAUGHING ELEPHANT

WWW.LAUGHINGELEPHANT.COM

PREFACE

The origins of my passion for tea began with a quote from Robert Frost: "Life is chaos, your duty is to make your own order, whether it be building a wall, plowing a field, or joining word to word." As a young woman I didn't fully appreciate Frost's words, but they inspired me to begin a lifelong search for my gift of ordering. I was invited, one Christmas, to a traditional afternoon tea with an English family of my acquaintance, which so delighted me that I bought some tea things and started giving teas for friends and family. Each time I enjoyed the experience more, and I finally realized that teatime was my calling.

I have a son and a daughter, and when they were 4 and 6 years old I started having tea with them every afternoon. We all enjoyed the preparations as well as the meal, and through the years the children learned much both about cooking and baking and of gentility and fellowship. The circle was completed when one birthday they gave me an exquisite tea-set, which I still use, to thank me for those peaceful afternoons.

I discovered that teatime calmed my children down. They enjoyed this serene, ordered part of the day. Children, for all their boisterousness, truly crave and are comforted by peaceful routines. Our conversation became ever more rewarding as they understood the civilized rhythm of our afternoon teas. Now they are married adults, they have each adopted the practice of regular afternoon teas with their children, and have observed that this draws the family nearer together and gives the children a deeper sense of order.

I have made an avocation of teaching others how to have tea. It is not difficult to learn, but for most Americans it needs to be demonstrated, more for the inner rhythm than for the simple practicalities. I visit schools, women's groups, clubs, and even prisons. Teatime does not always catch on after my demonstrations, but I receive many letters thanking me for the usefulness of what I introduced. The teatimes for children are the most successful. They are especially effective when the parents participate, and seem to become a part of many lives. It is this success that prompted me to write this book. My collection of teatime pictures is the heart of my teaching. If a reader will simply let these images sink into their consciousness, read my reflections of teatime and its uses, and follow my few simple instructions, then this pleasing custom can become a part of their and their children's lives.

Adult Teatime: The Model

The essence of teatime is, most importantly, a ritual. That tea is the usual beverage served is an historical accident – it could have been coffee or fresh-squeezed juices or cocoa. Teatime occurs for each family or group at a fixed time. The utensils are prescribed by tradition. The order of events does not vary. The offerings of food and drink are predictable. Women are almost always in charge, and pride themselves on the precision and consistency of their service. Genteel conversation is proper, and both sexes contribute equally. Seniority usually dictates who will pour, or "be Mum," though exceptions offer the delight of the unexpected.

Teatime is like a dance performed to a silent music. Those who perform a recurrent teatime find in it something of the satisfactions that musicians enjoy while performing familiar pieces. Teatime assures its devotees that whatever unpredictable things occur during the rest of the day, in this quiet ritual, order and quiet reassert themselves.

Children Having Tea With Adults

Growing up is largely a matter of imitation. Who knows what children would be like if they did not have adult examples before them? Speech is, of course, acquired by long years of imitation. How we move, eat, converse, play, and almost everything else we do is the result of watching others. Civilization is maintained by teaching.

In England, from the mid-nineteenth through the first half of the twentieth century, teatime was a central act of community learning. Here elders showed the young how important and satisfying were ritual and gentility. As children learn to talk by listening to their parents, children of this era learned their social graces by observation coupled with instruction. Now as then proper teatime etiquette is, fortunately, not very difficult nor very exacting to learn. Further, it offers immediate delight, even if one is only drinking, eating and watching.

Children Having Tea With Adults

Curtis Wager-Smith

HONOR C APPLETON

Tea with Pets, Dolls & Toys

A child's relations with pets and toys is of profound importance. Adults tend to underrate these bonds, and this deeply significant part of growing up is largely unexamined.

Children are under constant restraint. They take orders all day. Adults are in charge of their world. What a refreshment for them, then, is the situation with a pet! The child is in charge. The animal is to the child as the child is to the adult. How natural it is that pets should be invited to parties, and expected to behave.

Toys are even better. Pets have wills of their own, and are frequently slow to catch on. Toys are completely obedient. They sit where they are told. They respect their owner's every wish. Here the child is completely the master of the situation.

Having been taught the satisfactions of teatime, the child can enjoy the role of teacher, the leader who guides and instructs their students.

My dolly is giving a party
    Tomorrow at half-past four,
And she's sent an invitation
    To Peggy who lives next door;
And another to Peggy's dolly,
    So we shall be four at tea—
That really is one too many,
    As I've only got cups for three.

Mummy gave me a set last birthday,
    With a saucer for every cup,
But accidents seem to happen
    Whenever I'm washing-up.
I know they think I'm clumsy
    But they don't quite understand
No matter how tight you hold them,
    Things will slip out of your hand.

There'll be strawberry jam and honey
    And sugary buns and cake,
But nothing that's rich or heavy,
    To give the dollies an ache;
They're not a bit delicate really,
    They're as well as well can be,
But to run a risk would be silly,
    Both dolly and I agree.

This morning I cleaned the dolls' house,
    It took a long time to do;
I dusted the chairs and tables
    And polished the windows too.
So all will be clean and tidy
    From the roof to the kitchen floor,
When Peggy comes with her dolly
    To-morrow at half-past four.

Oh, we are so glad you're here!
    Now we'll all be gay and happy.
Let me introduce, my dear,
    Teddy, Tess, the Twins and Cappy.

Child Guests for Tea

Teatime, like all parties, is a chance for the hostess to show off. Children's tea-time is eminently such an occasion. The hostess pours. The hostess shows off her tea set, and displays, with flourishes, the skills she has learned. The invited children also find much to enjoy. As guests they enjoy the display and relish the refreshments.

Like most parties, teatime is reciprocal. You come to my house for tea, and I show you how well I enact it, and then I go to your house where you show me how fine your tea service is, and how skilled you are as a hostess.

Animals and toys are always welcome at these tea parties, for the more guests the deeper one's satisfaction as hostess.

Tea Party

▼ ▼ ▼

One, two,
Howdy-do!

Five, six,
The cake I'll fix!

Three, four,
You can pour!

Seven, eight,
Pass your plate!

Nine, ten,
Come again!

Outdoor Teas

Outdoor teas are teas of maximum freedom for children, for the house is the place of parental authority; as a child passes outdoors he partakes of greater freedom. Outdoors is a place of play and adventure, and teas under the open sky are less structured and more fun than any indoor tea.

It was customary, in the traditional English tea, to serve more fruit at outdoor teas. Sometimes, of course, fruit could be plucked directly from the garden or a nearby tree. An obvious advantage of the open-air tea party is the beauty of the surroundings. Given the vagaries of English weather they generally occurred in spring and summer, accompanied by blooming flowers, blossoming trees, bird song and gentle breezes.

Fantasy Tea Parties

Imagination is powerful in children, and the fictional characters they meet in books are powerful presences in their lives. It is only natural that they should want to invite these beings to their tea parties. Fairies were common in children's books of the late-19th and early-20th century. They were involved in every aspect of their dreaming and waking lives and were, naturally, invited to tea parties.

At an ordinary doll and toy tea, the playthings were immobile, but at a fantasy tea they gained the power of movement and could handle the teapot, cups and saucers by themselves.

Wild animals were frequent guests at teatime, and behaved themselves with appropriate decorum.

The most famous of all literary tea parties is the mad one from Alice's Adventures in Wonderland. This tea party was in the mind of every Victorian and Edwardian child, and helped to enlarge the concept of what a tea party could be.

THE DOLLIES HAVE A HAPPY LITTLE TEA PARTY.

Whom to Invite

As women were the true keepers of teatime in England, so girls are the likely teatime champions today. In almost every case a girl is the one who sets out to have a tea, and it follows that girls will usually be the ones invited. If a brother or other boy is invited he should be warned in advance that the whole thing is meant to be taken seriously, and that if he does not wish to enjoy a quiet and dignified repast he should decline the invitation.

Adults may properly be invited to a children's tea, and they will likely understand that they are there as guests, not as parents or other figures of authority.

No more than 6 guests should be invited.

Invitations

The formal and traditional nature of teatime points toward a formal and old-fashioned invitation. If not too burdensome, they are best hand written. Each invitation should be delivered in an envelope, formally addressed, such as:

Miss Priscilla Wiggins, at the house with the lilac bush
Or
Master Frank Taylor, at the domicile of brick

Here is a suggested form for an invitation:

MISS AMELIA LAWRENCE
Requests the pleasure of your company
at an afternoon tea
to be held between 4 and 5 o'clock pm
the afternoon of April 7
at 73 Holliday Drive
Please respond

What to Wear

Teatime is, for us, a formal and old-fashioned activity. In dressing for a tea one may make themselves formal and old-fashioned by simple means. A hat (as long as it is not a very casual one, such as a baseball cap) is a good start. A party dress is appropriate, and can be elaborated by the addition of a sash, shawl or scarf. A bracelet on the pouring wrist, which will be shown off during the tea service, adds to the hostess' glamour. We advise against borrowing mother's high-heeled shoes. These would make comic what should be quietly dignified. If in doubt prefer simplicity.

Teatime Etiquette

The essence of etiquette is kindness. The hostess of a tea party should always think what she can do to put her guests at ease. She must guard against growing too absorbed in the mechanism of tea serving lest she lose sight of her first duty as a hostess, which is to make her guests feel at home. If a spill or other accident occurs, she should make it seem unimportant.

Guests are under the obligation to make this a pleasant occasion for the hostess and the other guests. Conversation is a guest's chief duty. The best conversation is of interest to everyone at the party, and encourages everyone to join in. Shy children should make a real effort to be friendly, for shyness can be seen as indifference or even sullenness.

The Importance of Ceremony

Ceremony and ritual have a strong appeal for children, and they are usually willing to accommodate and cooperate in activities which partake of the ceremonial. Teatime can become such a ceremony, a time when manners are expected and the arts of conversation and cooperation practiced. To make teatime a compelling event, it is important to pay attention to the setting – to have special touches such as flowers, music, pretty table linens and special china, silver or what have you with which to serve the tea and its accompaniments. Children can then take pride in living up to the setting.

Having children help with setting the table, filling the milk pitcher and arranging the food attractively can also teach skills as well as investing the child in the rite of teatime. Older children can assist in food preparation, and helping to clean up afterwards is another valuable activity for all age groups.

Teatime Food

Teatime menus will, of course, vary according to the tastes of the children and the energy and wishes of the adults. Tea menus also vary with the season and setting. Winter teas tend to feature hot muffins or scones and warm cakes; outdoor teas of any season, but especially summer, include fresh fruit, cookies and sandwiches. A teatime menu can be anything from tea and toast to a full meal, as simple as a mother and daughter sitting at the kitchen table or as fancy as a birthday or Christmas tea with elaborate cakes and decorations. Included here are some of the foods and drinks traditional for English and American teas for children.

Some suggestions that require little preparation:

BREAD & BUTTER, TOASTED OR NOT, CAN BE CUT INTO DECORATIVE SHAPES
SMALL SANDWICHES ENGLISH MUFFINS
CRUMPETS OR SCONES CAKE
HARD-BOILED EGGS FRUIT
COOKIES, BOUGHT OR HOMEMADE, ESPECIALLY SHORTBREAD

SCONES

Preheat oven to 425°

Sift together:

1-3/4 CUPS ALL-PURPOSE FLOUR	1-1/2 TEASPOONS BAKING POWDER
1/2 TEASPOON SALT	1/4 CUP SUGAR

Cut into the above with pastry blender or two knives until the mixture looks like breadcrumbs:

1/2 STICK (2 OUNCES OR 1/4 CUP) BUTTER AT ROOM TEMPERATURE

Mix into the above until a soft dough is formed:

1 EGG BEATEN WITH ENOUGH HEAVY CREAM TO MEASURE 1/2 A CUP OF LIQUID.

Turn the dough out onto a floured surface and pat into a round 1/2 inch thick. You may cut the round into 12 triangles with a knife or cut into rounds with a glass or cookie cutter. Place on a greased and floured baking sheet. The unbaked scones may be glazed with an egg wash or cream and sprinkled with coarse sugar. Bake at 425° for 12 – 15 minutes or until scones have risen and are golden brown. Serve hot with preserves and butter or clotted cream.

CINNAMON TEA CAKE

Preheat the oven to 425°

Cream together:

1/2 CUP SUGAR	2 TABLESPOONS BUTTER, MELTED

Beat together and add to above:

1 EGG	1 CUP MILK

Mix together and add to above (mixing lightly, do not over mix):

1-1/4 CUPS ALL-PURPOSE FLOUR	2 TEASPOONS BAKING POWDER
1/4 TEASPOON SALT	

Spread evenly in an 8" greased and floured round cake pan.

Mix together and sprinkle on top of the batter:

3 TABLESPOONS SUGAR	2 TEASPOONS GROUND CINNAMON
3 TABLESPOONS SOFT BUTTER	1/4 CUP CHOPPED NUTS, IF DESIRED

Bake at 425° for 20-25 minutes or until a cake tester inserted near the center comes out clean, and serve hot.

GINGERBREAD

Preheat oven to 325°

Whisk together:

    1/2 CUP MOLASSES   1/2 CUP HONEY
    1 CUP BOILING WATER

Set aside to cool until warm.

Cream together:

    1 STICK (4 OUNCES OR 1/2 CUP) SALTED BUTTER AT ROOM TEMPERATURE
    2 TABLESPOONS SUGAR   1 EGG

Mix honey/molasses mixture into egg/sugar/butter mixture and stir until well-combined.

Sift together:

    2-1/2 CUPS ALL-PURPOSE FLOUR   1/2 TEASPOON BAKING SODA
    1/2 TEASPOON SALT   1 TEASPOON GROUND GINGER
    1 TEASPOON CINNAMON

Add to batter and stir until well combined.

Pour into greased and floured 9" square pan. Bake at 325° for 45-50 minutes or until a cake tester inserted near the center comes out clean. May be served hot, warm or at room temperature. Butter, whipped cream and ice cream are all delicious accompaniments.

LEMON SHORTBREAD

Preheat oven to 325°

Cream together:

    1 STICK (4 OUNCES OR 1/2 CUP) SALTED BUTTER AT ROOM TEMPERATURE
    4 TABLESPOONS SUGAR   FINELY GRATED ZEST OF 1 SMALL LEMON

Add to above:

    1 CUP ALL-PURPOSE FLOUR

Mix until it forms a soft dough. Divide in half and pat each half into a 6-7 inch round. Transfer rounds to a greased baking sheet. Score the shortbread into 6 pieces and decorate edges by pressing lightly all the way around with the tines of a fork.

Bake at 325° for 25-30 minutes or until the shortbread is just beginning to color at the edges. Cool for 5 minutes on pan, sprinkle with sugar if desired, then transfer to a wire rack to finish cooling. Snap into pieces along score lines to serve.

CUCUMBER SANDWICHES

    1 CUCUMBER, PEELED AND SLICED   12 SLICES OF THINLY-SLICED BREAD
    (If you use an English cucumber peeling is not necessary)
    UNSALTED BUTTER, ROOM TEMPERATURE   SALT
    PAPRIKA

Place cucumber slices between layers of paper towels to remove excess moisture

Butter the bread evenly and thinly. Cover 6 slices of bread with cucumber slices in 1 layer, sprinkle with salt, and cover with remaining 6 slices of bread.

Carefully cut the crusts from each sandwich with a sharp knife. Cut each sandwich into 4 like so –
X – or like so +.

Finished sandwiches look pretty sprinkled lightly with paprika

Place attractively on a plate and, if not serving immediately, cover with a tea towel or plastic wrap.

Yields 6 whole sandwiches or 24 fourths.

    VARIATIONS:

Butter may be seasoned with chopped mint or other herbs, or chopped watercress or sprouts

A mixture of butter and cream cheese may be used.

Mayonnaise may be used instead of butter.

Teatime Drinks

BLACK OR GREEN TEA

For children black and green teas should be weak.
1 or 2 teabags per pot steeped for 2 minutes should be
sufficient. Serve with milk (no milk with green tea) and
sugar or honey to taste. Thin slices of lemon should be
provided as well.

HERB TEAS

Peppermint, chamomile and fruit flavored herb teas are
good options for children. 2 teabags per pot, steeped for
4 – 6 minutes or according to particular tea's directions.
Serve with sugar or honey to taste.

CAMBRIC TEA

Named for an extremely thin cotton fabric, cambric tea is
training tea for children. It consists of nothing more than
a small amount of brewed tea (a tablespoon or so per
cup) mixed with equal parts hot water and milk, sugar to
taste.

ICED TEA

Iced tea is untraditional, but very welcome in hot weather.
Children will especially enjoy the novelty of making tea
using only solar energy.

SUN TEA

Fill a large glass container with filtered water. Add 1 teabag for every 2 cups of water used. Cover
and place in a sunny spot for three to five hours. Sun tea can be made with any type of tea and
tends to have a mild flavor. Serve over ice and garnish with lemon, lime or orange slices, or fresh
mint, with sugar to taste.

MILK, HOT CHOCOLATE AND OTHER BEVERAGES

Teatime for children really need not include tea. Any beverage enjoyed by children is suitable and
may be served from the teapot.

PICTURE CREDITS

Teatime Resources

TEAS & TEAWARE

REPUBLIC OF TEA – www.republicoftea.com

WHITTARD OF CHELSEA – www.whittard.co.uk

UPTON TEA IMPORTS – www.uptontea.com

TWININGS OF LONDON – www.shop.twiningsusa.com

PERENNIAL TEA ROOM – www.perennialtearoom.com

ORGANIC TEA

REMEDY TEAS – www.remedyteas.com

AMERICAN- MADE HANDCRAFTED TEA COZIES

CRICKLEWOOD COTTAGE – cricklewoodcottage@sbcglobal.net

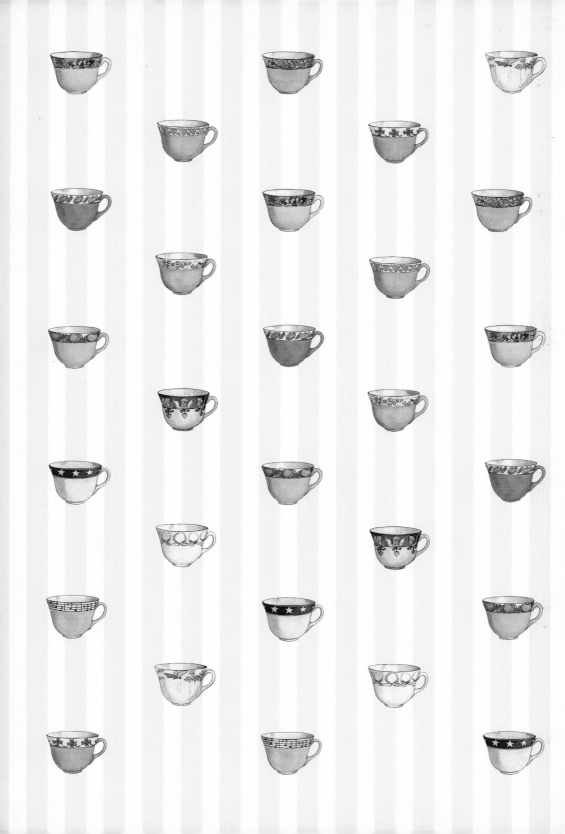